PASSIONS...

Golf

PASSIONS...

FOREWORD BY NICK FALDO
PHOTOGRAPHS BY MATTHEW HARRIS, THE GOLF PICTURE LIBRARY

DREAM PLACES YOU'D RATHER BE

DUNCAN BAIRD PUBLISHERS
LONDON

PASSIONS ... Golf

First published in the United Kingdom
and Ireland in 2005 by
Duncan Baird Publishers Ltd
Sixth Floor
Castle House
75–76 Wells Street
London W1T 3QH

Conceived, created and designed by
Duncan Baird Publishers

Copyright © Duncan Baird Publishers 2005
Text copyright © Duncan Baird Publishers 2005
Copyright of foreword © Nick Faldo 2005
Copyright of photographs © Matthew Harris
2005

All rights reserved. No part of this book may
be reproduced in any form or by any electronic
or mechanical means, including information
storage and retrieval systems, without permission in writing from the publisher, except by a
reviewer who may quote brief passages in a
review.

Managing Editor: Kirsten Chapman
Managing Designer: Manisha Patel
Picture Researcher: Louise Glasson

British Library Cataloguing-in-Publication Data:
A CIP record for this book is available from the
British Library

ISBN-10: 1-84483-172-8
ISBN-13: 9-781844-831722

10 9 8 7 6 5 4 3 2

Typeset in Bergell and Futura
Colour reproduction by Colourscan, Singapore
Printed in Singapore by Imago

Foreword

MAYBE I AM JUST A LITTLE BIT BIASED, BUT I HAVE ALWAYS RECKONED GOLF TO BE TRULY THE MOST GLOBAL AND THE MOST SPECTACULARLY COLOURFUL SPORT OF ALL. SO I AM VERY PLEASED TO PROVIDE A FOREWORD TO THIS PUBLICATION, *PASSIONS... GOLF*, PARTLY BECAUSE THE BOOK'S CONTENT PERFECTLY ILLUSTRATES MY CONTENTION, AND SECONDLY, BECAUSE THE MAIN CREATOR OF THIS WORK, MATTHEW HARRIS, IS SOMEONE WHOSE PHOTOGRAPHIC TALENT I HAVE LONG ADMIRED – AND SOMETIMES ENVIED.

6

THE LEGENDARY BROADCASTER HENRY LONGHURST WAS FOND OF SAYING, "GOLF TAKES US TO SUCH BEAUTIFUL PLACES." WELL, YOU ONLY HAVE TO FLICK THROUGH THE PAGES OF THIS BOOK TO SEE THAT IT ALSO GUIDES US TO SOME EXTRAORDINARY CORNERS OF THE WORLD. OVER THE YEARS, I HAVE BEEN FORTUNATE TO PLAY GOLF IN A GREAT VARIETY OF COUNTRIES AND AMID SOME DRAMATICALLY CONTRASTING ENVIRONMENTS – FROM THAILAND TO NEW ZEALAND AND FROM JAMAICA TO DUBAI. RECENTLY I HAVE ALSO BEEN INVITED TO DESIGN

GOLF COURSES IN SUCH DIVERSELY CHALLENGING LOCATIONS AS RUSSIA, THE DOMINICAN REPUBLIC, CAMBODIA AND DENMARK – ALTHOUGH, UNLIKE MATTHEW, I SEE, I STILL HAVE THE REMOTENESS OF GREENLAND TO EXPLORE!

ONE OF THE MOST SPECIAL PLACES TO PLAY GOLF IS IRELAND, SO I AM PLEASED THAT *PASSIONS... GOLF* INCLUDES A STRIKING AERIAL PHOTOGRAPH OF ONE OF MY FAVOURITE PARTS OF THE EMERALD ISLE, NAMELY BALLYLIFFIN IN COUNTY DONEGAL (PAGES 76-7). MATTHEW'S IMAGE HIGHLIGHTS THE GOLF

LINKS' REMARKABLE TERRAIN AND CAPTURES THE
MAGIC OF ITS SETTING. IT IS ONE OF SEVERAL
PICTURES THAT REMIND ME WHY I FEEL SO
PASSIONATE ABOUT THIS WONDERFUL GAME.

NICK FALDO

"Has anyone yet sung these delights of the game? ... the sense of freedom on a great expanse, the exhilaration, the vastness, the buoyancy, the exaltation?"

ARNOLD HAULTAIN (1857–1941)

> "There's such a simple satisfaction in the sound of the ball rolling into the cup."
>
> LEE FRENCH (1878–1965)

"Golf is not just an exercise; it's an adventure, a romance … a Shakespeare play in which disaster and comedy are intertwined."

HAROLD SEGALL (1897–1975)

"By nature, men are nearly alike; by practice, they get to be wide apart."

CONFUCIUS (551–479 BC)

"Our moments of inspiration are not lost ... for those experiences have left an indelible impression, and we are ever and anon reminded of them."

HENRY DAVID THOREAU (1817–62)

"Something about the sight of a fairway both soothes and excites me."

BOB CULLEN (1949–)

"Even when pushed to our limits of frustration, the focused beauty of a course can soothe and delight."

PHILIP MENDEZ (1921–79)

"Indeed, the highest pleasure of golf may be that on the fairways and far from all the pressures of commerce and rationality, we can feel immortal for a few hours."

COLMAN MCCARTHY (1933–)

"Stretch your lungs and your abilities on a rugged course beside the sea."

WALTER O'REILLY (1901–70)

"The positive thinker sees the invisible, feels the intangible and achieves the impossible."

CHARLES CALEB COLTON (1780–1832)

"Take risks: if you win, you will be happy; if you lose, you will be wise."

PROVERBIAL WISDOM

"We do not remember days,
we remember moments."

CESARE PAVESE (1908–50)

"The well-resolved mind is single and one-pointed."

BHAGAVAD GITA (C. 4TH–3RD CENTURY BC)

"Beauty of style, harmony, grace and good rhythm depend on simplicity."

PLATO (429–347 BC)

"You already possess everything necessary to become great."

NATIVE AMERICAN MAXIM

"There are complete men and incomplete men. If you would be a complete man, put all of your soul's strength into all of your life's actions."

EUGENIO MARIA DE HOSTOS (1839–1903)

"The only thing a golfer needs is more daylight."

BEN HOGAN (1912–97)

"This time, like all times, is a very good one, if we but know what to do with it."

RALPH WALDO EMERSON (1803–82)

Locations

page 5 13th hole (par 5), Augusta National, USA
pages 10–11 3rd hole (par 4), Machrihanish, Scotland
pages 12–13 16th hole (par 3), Troon North, USA
page 14 1st hole (par 4), Tehàma, USA
pages 16–17 16th hole (par 4), The K Club, Ireland
page 19 16th hole (par 4), Milnerton, South Africa
pages 20–21 10th hole (par 5), Furnace Creek, USA
page 22 16th hole (par 4), Oakland Hills, USA
pages 24–25 13th hole (par 5), Ballyliffin (Glashedy), Ireland
pages 26–27 17th hole (par 4), Cypress Point, USA
page 29 14th hole (par 3), Bridport and West Dorset, England
pages 30–31 17th hole (par 3), PGA National, USA
pages 32–33 10th hole (par 4), Ballybunion (Old), Ireland
page 34 Silhouette of a golfer
pages 36–37 18th hole (par 5), Reflection Bay, USA
pages 38–39 2nd hole (par 5), Archerfield Links (Fidra), Scotland
page 40 6th hole (par 4), Rye, England

pages 42–43 3rd hole (par 3), Desert Mountain, USA
pages 44–45 7th hole (par 4), St Andrews Bay, Scotland
page 47 18th hole (par 4), Cypress Point, USA
pages 48–49 17th hole (par 3), Cabo del Sol, Mexico
page 50 16th hole (par 4), Leopard Rock, Zimbabwe
pages 52–53 3rd hole (par 5), Kiawah Island (The Ocean), USA
pages 54–55 1st hole (par 4), Mid Ocean Club, Bermuda
page 57 15th hole (par 4), Doonbeg, Ireland
pages 58–59 17th hole (par 3), Atlanta Athletic Club, USA
pages 60–61 Cold morning start, Hayling Island, England
page 62 Aerial view, Emirates Golf Club, United Arab Emirates
pages 64–65 8th hole (par 4), Shadow Ridge, USA
pages 66–67 10th hole (par 4), Lost City, South Africa
page 68 Ice golf, Greenland
pages 70–71 Archerfield Links (Fidra), Scotland
pages 72–73 18th hole (par 5), Doral (Blue Monster), USA
page 74 15th hole (par 3), Valderrama, Spain
pages 76–77 Aerial view, Ballyliffin, Ireland
pages 78–79 8th hole (par 3), Erinvale, South Africa
page 80 18th hole (par 5), Pebble Beach, USA

pages 82–83 3rd hole (par 5), Naples, USA
pages 84–85 13th hole (par 4), Nefyn, Wales
page 87 1st hole (par 4), Pasatiempo, USA
pages 88–89 4th hole (par 3), Royal County Down, Ireland
pages 90–91 15th hole (par 3), Selborne, South Africa
page 93 7th hole (par 3), Vale do Lobo, Portugal
pages 94–95 5th hole (par 4), Royal Dornoch, Scotland
pages 96–97 18th hole (par 5), Palm Meadows, Australia
page 98 13th hole (par 3), Taiheiyo, Japan
pages 100–101 8th hole (par 4), Machrie, Scotland
page 103 10th hole (par 4), Turnberry (Ailsa), Scotland
pages 104–105 5th hole (par 5), New South Wales Golf Club, Australia
page 106 5th hole (par 4), Sandy Hills, Ireland

Text credits

The publishers would like to thank the following for permission to reproduce their copyright material. Every care has been taken to trace copyright owners, but if we have omitted anyone we apologize and will, if informed, make corrections in any future edition.

page 15 Arnold Haultain, from *The Mystery of Golf* (Houghton Mifflin, 1908).
page 41 Bob Cullen, from *Why Golf?* (Simon & Schuster, 2002).
Copyright © Bob Cullen, 2002
page 51 Colman McCarthy, from *The Pleasures of the Game* (Dial Press, 1977)
Copyright © Colman McCarthy, 1977

About the contributors

NICK FALDO, FOREWORD

With more than 40 tournament victories worldwide, Nick Faldo is one of the greatest golfers of all time. He has claimed three US Masters titles and three British Open Championships, and holds the Ryder Cup record for most appearances (11) and most points won (25). In 2008 he will captain the European Ryder Cup team at Valhalla in Kentucky, USA. Over the last ten years, Nick Faldo has also established himself as one of the world's foremost golf course architects. His company, Faldo Design, has created award-winning layouts in such diverse places as China, Germany, Australia, the USA, Vietnam and Canada.

MATTHEW HARRIS, PHOTOGRAPHER

Matthew Harris is an award-winning golf photographer whose work has taken him to 44 countries around the world. He has covered 82 major championships and Ryder Cups since 1984, and is the founder of The Golf Picture Library (TGPL).

All pictures by Matthew Harris, The Golf Picture Library (TGPL)